3

DEDICATION

Years after writing some of these stories I became involved in the world of hospice; first as a hospice volunteer and later in a hospice singing choir. I saw first hand the beauty and the power of people at the end of life, and it helped to alleviate some of the fear of dying.

This book is dedicated to the past and present members of the Harbour Singers Choir in Saco, Maine, and to all of the hospice workers and members of hospice singing choirs - the volunteer angels that sit and/or sing with us at the end of our lives.

Blessings,
D'Vorah

AN ATTITUDE OF GRATITUDE

I offer my heartfelt gratitude to:

Leela Elizabeth Kelley, my amazing daughter. I owe her a huge debt of gratitude for leading the way even back then – she is still one of my best teachers;

Cherryl Jensen, Amherst Writers and Artists (AWA) facilitator, whose love of writing was evident in the way she facilitated those early groups, giving feedback and encouragement to fledgling writers. It was in Cherryl's group that the first of these stories arrived;

Diana Damato, AWA facilitator, whose gentle guidance encouraged me to keep going, and who always led by example. Within the circle that Diana led, the last story emerged;

All the men and women who sat in all the many writing circles I've had the good fortune to be part of, for their creativity, honesty, deep sharing, vulnerability, patience, encouragement, feedback, and wisdom;

Geralyn St. Joseph, proofreader and friend, without whom this book would still be just on my computer;

Judy Campbell, who gave me the benefit of her wisdom in navigating the publishing world;

And to Nancy and Steve Durkee, my aunt and uncle, who always encouraged me to stretch out of my comfort zone; they will be reading these from "the other side" – I miss them both so very much.

Let life be as beautiful as summer flowers
And death as beautiful as autumn leaves.
~Rabindranath Tagore

<u>Sunset Voices</u>, thirty-three fictional accounts of people nearing the end of their lives, are snapshots of not just death and dying, but of living and how we create a storehouse of memories.

As a hospice volunteer and a member of a Hospice singing group, I saw first hand the beauty and the power of people at the end of life. As an ordained Interfaith Minister who has officiated at memorial services, I know the importance of creating space for the stories to emerge. As a woman in the last third of my life, I believe that we can learn to more fully appreciate our lives by embracing our mortality, and offer these "snapshots" as a way to do so.

I offer them because to not do so might leave the world bereft of compassion for those at the end of their lives: their stories deserve to be told. And because . . ."I have no choice; there are stories knocking at the door."

Many blessings to you who have purchased this book – may it bring you peace and a greater understanding that we are all part of the great circle of life.

D'Vorah Kelley

http://www.revdvorah.com

rev.dvorah@gmail.com

TABLE OF CONTENTS

7

SUNSET VOICES

INTRODUCTION
Why I Wrote These Stories

"If you cannot find your tongue do not look for it
for if you are so busy looking it cannot find you
the doves are getting dizzy and your grandmother's annoyed
be still and let them find you
they will come when they are ready."
Excerpt from "If You Lose Your Pen" by Ruth Foreman in
We Are the Young Magicians
http://www.ruthforman.com/publications/we-are-young-magicians/

I Write Because. . .

I write because . . .

"the doves are getting dizzy and your grandmother's annoyed" because they expect nothing less from me than channeling and witnessing the stories of men and women from another dimension.

I write because . . .

there are stories that only I can tell, and if I do not tell them, they will sit on the shelf gathering dust. Only the spiders and mice will notice them, and they are too busy weaving webs and gathering food to care.

10

I write because . . .

> of shawls and parasols, secrets and spaces, jars of life and Rumi's wisdom, whistling tea kettles and river boats, the seashore and rules, fresh hay and runaways. Because of whispers in my mind, that want to be brought into the Light of Day. A promise fulfilled.

I write because . . .

> their voices need to be heard. Matthew's, Sarah's, Carl's, Thea's, Mary's, Maude's, Rob's, Josephine's and all the others. Clamoring softly to be heard, seen and known. Remembered.

I write because . . .

> to not write the stories might leave the world bereft of compassion for those at the end of their lives. Heartache and joy, laughter and tears, grief and humor, and most of all love – a recipe for Life as I follow the words at the end of my pen.

I write because . . .

> I have no choice; there are stories knocking at the door. My pen leaks onto the page, a flood of words appears, and I am powerless to stop them.

I invite you on a journey as you listen to the voices of people in their sunset years. May they touch your heart as they have touched mine.

Matthew
Morning At the Cape

 Half an hour before sunrise, and already the horizon was kissed with golden rosy light. It was a beautiful way to start his last day on earth, not that Matthew knew that, as he watched a lone seagull patrolling the shoreline in the early morning calm.

He'd been restless, even in his dreams, a night spent waking and looking at the glow of the digital clock on his nightstand. Finally, with a quiet sigh, he resigned himself to the fact that sleep, really deep sleep, was an elusive memory, a thing of the past, and so he rose, a half an hour before sunrise.

Matthew had been a night owl most of his seventy-two years. It was only recently, since moving to the Cape, to their retirement home and a slower paced life - on doctor's orders - that he'd begun making friends with the sunrise, not always by choice.

Slipping his bare feet into well-worn, scruffy slippers and pulling the belt of his terry-cloth robe snug against his belly, he wandered out onto the deck overlooking the harbor. He'd taken time, of course, to make a cup of strong coffee. If he couldn't sleep, at least he'd wake up properly, he thought to himself as he watched the morning come creeping over the masts of the sailboats moored at Bates Marina. Sipping his coffee, he thought of the game he and Shirley used to play. They loved to create stories about the people who owned the boats, the yachts, cabin cruisers, even the smaller sailboats that took up little room among the giants. They'd only had a little over a year here together, and this morning was the first time in the six months since she'd died, that he'd found himself creating a story about one of the boats and the people who were aboard.

"Life does go on, doesn't it old girl?" He spoke as he often did, as if Shirley were there to listen.

The coffee needed freshening and he needed a shower, but the peace of the morning was not to be denied. So Matthew waited, just waited, an impatient man learning patience at last.

Katherine
No Songs Now

Alpha Images. The ones that used to be on top, the important ones that had played over and over in Katherine's mind, taking root, burrowing in deeper, ever deeper until they became ever so subtle ghosts, wispy shadows of their former selves, all she had left.

Mixed in among the shadows she found the remnants of a borrowed love poem, written when she had been sixteen and in love with life and all its promises. She remembered, on the infrequent good days, that the boy had been at camp with her that summer, worshiped from afar, her love never declared. She, in her despair, had turned to the poets in her sophomore English class to soothe her troubled soul.

Another shadow fluttered just out of reach, an alpha image conveyed to her in graduate school. Katherine had been a music major, with the voice of an angel, destined for greatness; everyone had said so.

"All art," her voice teacher had declared solemnly one day, as if imparting truth with a capital T, "all art leads to song. Only song has the power to make grown men cry." As if that explained everything.

The remnants, the shadows of those former alpha images, came less frequently now. These days, she passed most of her waking time engaging everyone who would listen in her relentless questioning, wringing a lace handkerchief, as if seeking to wring out her pain.

"Why?" she would beseech the nurses, the other patients, even visitors caught unawares. "Why did we take our children to Ireland?"

It never did any good to attempt to answer her; she'd be on to the next person, a tear or two finding their way down her wrinkled cheeks. There were no songs on her lips now, only one unanswerable question.

Julius
Mama's Pride

Julius was near the end of his life.

He'd made the decision to die, to let go, just stop the dialysis that had been keeping him alive all these many months. Not that it had been an easy, instantaneous decision. It hadn't, but he felt in his bones that he was almost ready. Almost, but not quite.

The nursing home was quiet tonight, and as he closed his eyes, he saw the face of his wife Mary. Her way to heaven had been quick - gone before she could even call out, just after dinner several years ago.

After the funeral, Julius had gathered up her silver hairbrush, comb, and mirror from the top of her bureau, where it had held a place of honor for over fifty years. He knew the girls had no doubt wondered where the silver set had gone. After all, it had rested for years on top of the ancient lace cloth that had come  over on the ship from Ireland with their great-grandmother. But they had never asked, and Julius had never volunteered the information.

The silver set and the lace, known in the family as "Mama's pride," were linked in Julius's mind with the image of his wife's careful brushing of her once auburn

17

tresses, which had thinned and become silver as she aged. One hundred strokes every night of their married life, never missing one night until that last one.

The brush, even now, held strands of her hair, as if she'd just finished brushing it.

Julius, mindful of the nurses down the hall, crept out of bed and moved cautiously and slowly towards his bureau. He opened the bottom drawer and carefully removed a silver box, inlaid with Mother-of-Pearl, and wrapped in a soft cotton cloth. He'd managed to keep it hidden from the girls and the nurses; his secret.

Tears crept down his cheeks as he lovingly opened the box. Not bothering to wipe them away, he took out the priceless treasures and arranged them on the lace cloth that had lain at the bottom of the box. He smiled, and crept back into bed, pulling the cotton blanket up over his tired, worn out body.

He was ready now, ready to finally join Mary.

Sarah
Jars of Life

There was a time, oh so long ago, when Sarah made numerous trips each fall down the well-worn cellar stairs, to the root cellar tucked away in the back of the dirt basement. "Jars of Life" she'd called them, the neatly labeled, alphabetically arranged rows of peaches, pickles, beets, tomatoes, beans and more. Oak bins, made by her husband's calloused hands, held a winter's supply of tree-ripened sweet apples, Russet potatoes and several varieties of winter squash. Those gifts from the earth, harvested and put by in the lingering warmth of late fall, had held a glimmer of that warmth, even down there in the coolness of the root cellar.

Sarah no longer ventured down those steps, hadn't in years too many to count. She lay, day after endless day, in the nursing home, oblivious to her sterile surroundings. Her ancient eyes, eyes that had once twinkled at the antics of her four children and grandchildren, were now blinded by cataracts as thick as the panes of glass in the window high up on one wall of the old root cellar. Her hair, once luxurious and honey colored, now wispy strands of gray, clung to her forehead in much the same manner as the wisps of cobwebs now clung to the once pristine shelves, upon which the memories of the remnants of the Jars of Life still echoed.

Instead of fresh, sun-filled fruits and vegetables gathered by her own hands, Sarah's meals were bland, mostly liquid, nothing in which anyone would ever delight. Every now and then a ghost of a smile would dimple her cheeks, giving the nurses a glimpse of the woman she had once been.

Beneath the quiet exterior, worn down by time, the blood in her veins still coursed strong and vital, as it had in the days when as a young wife and mother she had taken such pride in her canning and preserving. Why, she'd won a blue ribbon three years in a row for her sweet pickles! Those ribbons had gone the way of so many things in her life, lost and forgotten as Sarah herself now was. She had outlived her husband, her children, her friends, and even her precious root cellar. Now, she simply waited for her turn to enter the great mystery.

Grace
Unlimited Love

 They held hands, that last time together. Grace's were paper thin, light as a feather resting in Laura's. Her whole body was thin, as if her spirit were already disappearing from the body and returning home.

At one point in that last afternoon that they spent together, Grace, shaking her head with as much force as she could muster, had declared with a show of her old self, "I AM NOT SICK! I hate that everyone thinks I'm sick. One or two parts don't work, but I'm still me!"

Laura, still holding Grace's hands, sang to her; they'd always had the connection of their love of music, and it was a gift she could offer. Ever so slightly, Grace squeezed Laura's hand as the song slowly ended, smiled her sweet smile, and closed her eyes, bathed in the words and the love behind them.

At her memorial service, her husband, her children, and longtime friends spoke of her huge, giving heart. She was the most nurturing person most of them had known - a generous, loving spirit.

When it was Laura's turn, she shared a heart-wrenching thought she'd had as she drove down to the

Cape from Maine. Quietly, looking intently at those gathered in the small church, she asked the questions that had been bothering her.

"Had all of us, loving her as we had, sucked her dry so that her life force diminished decades before it should have? Do we really have an unlimited supply of love?"

In the silence that followed, it came to her, the answer. It came to her in Grace's voice, with great certainty.

"I believe we do. I believe it may be the only unlimited thing we have."

Muriel
Wildflowers

At the end of her life, Muriel rises in the morning stiff and creaky and makes her way slowly to the bathroom. Many years before, after she and Bernie had been  in the house for several years, she had redone the tiny room in shades of blue and yellow, with wildflowers scattered on the white tiles. Bernie, God rest his soul, had thought it frivolous to spend hard earned money on painted ceramic tiles. "Pure foolishness, woman!" he'd exclaimed when he saw them.

Muriel had found a mirror at Johnson's Bed and Bath Shop out on the old Richmond Highway. Besides the wildflowers tiles, it was her favorite find. It had a white pine frame and a multifaceted glass knob that sparkled like new after Muriel cleaned it with vinegar. At the bottom was a place to hang a hand towel, and she'd splurged when she'd found one with almost the same wildflowers as were on the tiles.

They hadn't had much money back then, but she had saved her money made selling eggs along with fresh vegetables from her garden and had delighted in the small bathroom's restoration. Bernie might have thought it foolish, but he had grown to enjoy the wildflowers and the mirror, not that he had ever said so outright. But she could tell.

As Muriel makes her way into the bathroom and stands in front of the mirror, she smiles at herself, as she does every morning now. Several years before, a hairline crack had appeared on the mirror's smooth surface. She had watched as over time, faint spidery cracks had flowed across the surface, winter's ice at spring's thaw.

Her smile is an easy, gentle one. She smiles at the poetry of the lines chiseled onto the face of the mirror, thinking that they reflect and capture the lines that have slowly appeared on her face. "The mirror and I are aging together," she thinks, comforted by the thought.

On her way out of the bathroom, after switching off the light bulb that hangs from the ceiling - Bernie had always promised her a new light fixture to match the new bathroom - she pauses in the doorway, readying herself for what the day will bring.

Gwen
Shawls and Parasols

The white wicker chair, a gray shawl draped casually over one arm as if its owner had come home in a hurry, sat in front of the sun-filled window in the bedroom. A white umbrella, the kind used to shield against the sun, not the rain, lay propped against the arm of the chair.

Next to the chair sat a small wooden desk, the kind with a miniature, hidden drawer. A simple vase filled with pansies rested on top of the desk. It was a time-honored tradition to always have fresh flowers in that vase, a tradition still fulfilled by the family, even now.

The room held an air of expectancy, of a breath being held in anticipation. In this room, Gwen had welcomed her new husband into her arms, had birthed all three of her children, had nursed her husband John through his final illness and had now herself lain silent and weak, surrounded by her children and grandchildren as the end neared.

The wicker chair had been part of a set that her children had given their parents for their fortieth wedding anniversary. The other chair, along with the matching couch and coffee table, still graced the side porch. Gwen had early on claimed one of the chairs, with its bright flowered cushion, for her bedroom reading chair when that room had been redone. She had loved sitting there with a cup of tea and a good book in the quiet afternoon while John was at work. After he retired and was underfoot all the time, it became an unspoken agreement that he would not disturb her time in the chair.

The gray, lacy shawl had been made for her by her eldest granddaughter, Lydia, when she was first learning to knit. "Look Gram," she had exclaimed proudly. "I made it myself, just for you!" Gwen had made all the appropriate grandmotherly noises and had overlooked the dropped stitches and the less than perfect edges. The shawl had been the perfect size and weight for those afternoon teas, keeping small drafts from chasing down her back. Even when she had no longer been able to leave the bed, the hospice worker would bring her the shawl and gently wrap it around her frail shoulders. Gwen would sigh quietly, her bony, gnarled hands resting lightly on top of it.

The parasol, for that's what it was, hadn't been used in years. Cindy, her great-granddaughter, had found it in Gwen's closet when she was visiting. She brought it out, laughing as she opened it up and asked, "Gram, whatever did you use this for? It's cloth and way too pretty to be used as an umbrella!"

Gwen had smiled and in a whispery voice told Cindy that, "all genteel ladies in Newport carried parasols to protect their skin from the sun." Cindy, who spent part of her paycheck at the tanning salon, thought that deliciously old-fashioned and quaint, and couldn't wait to tell her friends. She had leaned it against the chair and gone over to sit with her grandmother and read to her from one of her favorite books.

In the days and weeks that had followed, the parasol had leaned, forgotten, against the chair, as if keeping watch. Dust had collected on its ruffles, a relic of the past, part of Gwen's past, a part of no one's future.

Olivia
Secrets and Spaces

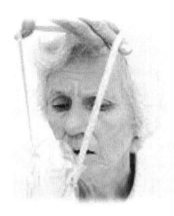

Olivia knew about secrets, knew about holding them close to her breast as if they were a fledgling bird. But what did she know about spaces? Only this – that there are spaces that hold the secrets, secrets from the past that need to breathe in the present moment.

Breaths came harder to her now, the oxygen mask covering her face like a necessary intruder. But then, hadn't she worn a mask all the days of her life? It would not do to let people in, let them see who she really was, or so she had always believed.

She had worn many masks in her lifetime – the mask of the dutiful daughter, the mask of the proper wife to her lawyer husband, the mask of the responsible and doting mother to her three children, and now, the mask of death lay waiting to be worn – her last mask, the one she would wear to meet her maker.

"Hell no!" she thought rebelliously, "Hell and damnation! I'm ninety-three years old and I'm tired of being who others think I am!

And she made space, in the last moments of her life, for the Truth of her Self to shine through. She died with a smile on her lips, the oxygen mask dangling from her hand.

Colette
Life On Her Terms

Colette never assumed that people wanted to hear what she had to say. But that never stopped her. She just looked them in the eye and spoke what was on her mind, consequences be damned. It was the guiding principle in her life,"to thine own self be true", and while it had often landed her in hot water, it had also served her well over the years. First as a journalist in her native France, covering the political scene, and later when she moved to Washington D.C. and covered American politics for the <u>Washington Post</u>.

She had published three biographies of famous people that had been fairly well received, although one reviewer had chastised her for her "outspoken contempt for her subject," which Colette received as high praise.

She always lived life to the fullest, on her terms, and with no regrets. No husband, but plenty of satisfied lovers. No children or pets to clutter her flamboyant life. She had traveled extensively, dined with the rich and famous, and laughed when people suggested that at 82 she should slow down.

"Plenty of time for slowing down when I'm in my grave," was her retort, delivered in a voice made husky from too many late nights and too many cigarettes over the last 60 years.

So it came as no surprise that when the time came, Colette looked Death in the face, laughed out loud, saying, "It's been a hell of a ride! I guess it's finally time to start that slowing down shit that people were always chiding me about."

Life, and death, on her terms. That was certainly a fitting epitaph for a crusty old lady from France!

WHAT YOU SEEK...
IS ALSO SEEKING YOU
—RUMI

Carl
Rumi's Wisdom

"Seek the wisdom that will untie your knot
Seek the path that will demand your whole being.
Leave that which is not, but appears to be,
Seek that which is, but is not apparent."
Rumi

Funny how some things come back to you. Carl hadn't thought of this poem for years but had come across it while cleaning out some of his old papers in preparation for putting his house on the market and moving into an assisted living facility.

He had first heard it as an undergrad at Harvard Business School when an English professor quoted it and then wrote it on the board for extra emphasis on the importance of Rumi's words. Carl had copied the poem into his notebook, so as to be ready if it showed up on a test.

It has always been assumed by his family that Carl would follow in his grandfather and father's chosen profession and become a lawyer. His path had been laid out for him since childhood, and up to a point, he had followed it without question, though even then it was not what he really wanted to do.

Following graduation from Bentley University in Boston, he had applied and been accepted to Harvard Law School. From there, he was destined to enter the law Office of Shelton and Sons, wear a suit and tie every day, marry a woman of whom his family approved, have the prescribed 2.5 children, and grow old and retire from the family firm. That had always appeared to be his path, but at a pivotal point in his life, he had left that safe and secure path and ventured into the unknown. And, as Robert Frost had written, that had made all the difference.

That safe path had changed during his last semester in Law School; it changed the night he met James. He had not even wanted to go to the party, but his roommates thought he needed a night away from studying, so he went. And while not apparent that night, fate was changing the game plan.

Carl had noticed James, but then, at 6'4" it was hard not to notice him, especially in his "Bohemian artist's attire". Carl never could recall how they'd started talking, but two hours later, they were still talking, oblivious to the rest of the guests.

Over the next few months, the two young men spent quite a bit of time together; drinks, dinner, movies, long walks along the Charles River, and afternoons spent in James' studio loft in Cambridge. Their mutual attraction was disquieting, to say the least, but too strong to ignore. Finally, they realized that they could no longer deny their love.

Carl sighed when he remembered the scene in his family's living room the night he and James told them they were in love and planning to move in together. And he suspected that what was worst for his father was to be told that Carl no longer planned to be a lawyer, but was instead following a long-buried desire to work with his hands.

He rubbed his hands along the breakfront he had made with such loving care all those years ago. They were good years, with lots of good memories, but now, with James' passing six months ago, Carl was ready to move on, alone.

He found himself rereading the poem, chuckling as he realized the connection to his life with what Rumi was writing about. He had had the wisdom, or maybe it was good luck, to have found the path that he could live with his whole being, and with love. He knew he was a lucky man, and his heart was filled with gratitude.

Gladys
The Day the Music Stopped

"When I was young, I danced my way through life. Perpetual motion, that was me – much to my very proper mother's dismay. My steps were full of springtime gladness, even in the midst of cold New England winters. Daffodils, crocus, March peepers, returning Robins – they all became partners in the dance, and I loved every minute of it!"

A tear trickled down Gladys' cheek as she spoke. Susan, her hospice volunteer, gently wiped away the wetness, and then settled back in her chair, holding Gladys' paper-thin hand in her own. She had brought some music today, hoping it would stir Gladys out of her lethargy. She was gratified to see that it had worked, as Gladys usually did not talk very much during her visits. The music had obviously stirred up some memories long forgotten by the old woman.

"Tell me more, Gladys," Susan prompted her gently. "Tell me more about dancing when you were young."

Another tear slowly leaked out of the corner of Gladys' eye. Then another, and another, until there was a steady stream coursing down the deep valleys in her cheeks, unchecked. Suddenly, she clutched Susan's hand tightly and tried to blink the tears away.

"I remember the day I stopped dancing. The day the music went out of my life." She paused, then continued, her voice heavy with sadness. "It was the day my baby died. He was only two weeks old, and never had a chance to dance. I never could bear to dance after that."

Closing her eyes she paused again for a few moments. Susan thought she had fallen asleep, but then Gladys opened her eyes, turned her head and looked directly at Susan. A tremulous smile crossed her lips, as she whispered, "Thank you. I've waited all this time, wasted all this time, but today I heard the music again, and I know I will be dancing again, very soon now." Her smile deepened. "And my baby will be with me again, and we will dance together, and it will be perpetual springtime."

And then it was Susan's turn to weep.

Henry
The Old Tractor

The old John Deere tractor rested in the tall grass, weed-covered, rusty, and forgotten. It had been years since it had been a useful part of farm life. Mice had made their homes up under the hood, a family of raccoons at one time had taken up residency under the tractor, and the old leather seat was cracked and worn.

In much the same way, Henry lay in his bed, surrounded by memories of the past. There were pictures of his children sitting on the tractor during planting season. He had outlived three of his five children, and the other two lived too far away to visit. He didn't even really know any of his eight grandchildren, city dwellers all of them. The Christmas cards sent to him over the years had been their only connection, a reminder of what might have been, if he hadn't been so stubborn.

In one of his favorites, Molly, his wife of fifty-seven years, smiled out at him – sitting on the front porch shelling peas, a shy smile the only indication that she knew she was being captured on film. Oh, how he missed her!

And there were books - so many books. Henry had always loved to read, but life on a farm didn't allow much free time for reading. So after Molly died, and he'd had the stroke that had landed him in the Easy Rest Nursing Home, he'd bugged anyone who would listen to bring him something to read. He said that reading took him away from himself, opened up a world of possibilities far away from the life he'd known as a farmer, a husband or a father.

Now the books were covered in dust. His hands, once so big they could grab a bale of hay and swing it up into the hayloft, now shrunken to half their size, lay on the plain green blanket, too weak to hold a book, much less a bale of hay.

Henry and the tractor had both outlived their usefulness on the farm, both worn out by the passing of time.

Thea
The Patchwork Sweater

It is a crisp fall day, the kind of day that New Englanders take a personal pride in, as if Mother Nature presents such a bountiful display just for them. Thea has seen more autumnal colors than she can remember, stretching all the way back to when she shuffled through the leaves on her way to Miss Shelley's kindergarten class at Franklin Elementary School, tagging along after Jimmy and Frankie, her older brothers.

Jimmy and Frankie had both died years earlier, Jimmy in the Korean War, and Frankie as he played golf at the Fairhaven Country Club. Sometimes Thea sits and looks at their photographs on the bookshelf in her small room, trying to remember their voices, trying to remember them. So much is slipping away, almost on a daily basis. So she sits and tries to hold onto memories.

But she still manages to put on a brave face, complete with her trademark rouge and red lipstick. Mother always gave her grief about it. "Cynthea, you look like a cheap honky-tonk girl with all that redness," she would say, one hand on her heart, as if Thea would be the death of her. Mother always called her Cynthea.

Today, knowing there would be a tangy bite in the air later in the morning, Thea puts on her favorite sweater, the one the twins had given her for Christmas one year, thinking that she'd probably never wear it. But wear it she does, with a twinkle in her eyes when she sees the looks people in the town give her. She is sure the stories have managed to find their way to the younger generation, to whom her escapades must seem tame and trivial if they even give any thought to them at all.

Ah, but in her day, oh yes, in her day, she'd ----but whatever thoughts she is thinking tumble away from her as they are wont to do these days. Sometimes she hears her mother's voice in her head clearer than she hears her own thoughts. So much is slipping away from her, little by little she is losing herself, the self she took such pride in being, as exhausting as it was at times to swim upstream, against the current. Not a proper girl at all. Thea giggles as this thought comes to her, in her mother's voice. No, not a proper girl at all!

With that thought, dressed in her patchwork sweater that even today gives Mother Nature a run for her money, Thea heads down to the dining room, ready for another day of trying to remember who she used to be.

Claire
The Mirror

Claire knew she had to face her fears. Not because her therapist told her it would make the time she had left more meaningful, more precious. Not because her children deserved a legacy of truth from their mother. Not because her church admonished, in the Tiffany window behind the altar, that "the Truth Shall Make You Free."

The truth, her truth, might set her free of the crippling fears that had clung to her, sometimes like a shroud, heavy and dark. At other times, her fears sat on her tongue, metallic and bitter, waiting to swallow her whole. She had lived with this relentless companion for so long that she had difficulty imagining her life without its shadowy presence.

 The thought of her fears being a shadow gave her pause. Grasping her cane firmly, she lifted herself out of the chair, and slowly made her way to the mirror sitting on her bureau. Holding it close, she stood for several minutes, studying her image very intently. Suddenly, and much to her surprise, she began to chuckle, then laughed out loud as she watched the old lady in the mirror.

Hearing her, Claire's daughter rushed into her mother's room, in time to hear her say to the image in the

41

mirror, "Jokes on me, you old fool. No shadow, nothing there but me."

"Mom, mom, are you okay? Whatever are you doing? Come on, let's get you back to bed."

Claire reached out and touched her daughter's cheek.

"Call your brother and sister and ask them to come over. We need to talk. There's something I should have told you all years ago."

Claire looked back at her image in the mirror, and smiled, and her image self smiled back, at peace at last.

Mary
Coming Home

The room seemed smaller than she'd remembered it, but then, she was smaller, just a shadow of her former self. She was grateful, so very grateful to be here. There had been so many days when gratitude was hard to come by, when tears replaced the familiar smiles and laughter for which she'd always been known. Yes, she knew that others had walked this path, partaken of this particular journey, but that didn't necessarily make it easier.

She sighed as she looked around the room, with its bright blue and yellow curtains that matched the lighter yellow of the walls. It was a cheerful room, such a comfortable room. Sitting in the rocker, she thought about  the strange phone call that had led her here, back to her childhood hometown just outside Burlington Vermont.

The small town of Jericho was much the same as she'd remembered it, the quintessential New England village, with its village green and obligatory white-steeple church, the church she been married in, and from which she'd left Jericho, never to return, until yesterday.

The phone call had come just hours after the doctors at Beth Israel had told her that they had run out of options.

"Your cancer has spread to your liver and bones," Dr. Milo had pronounced, touching her hand lightly as he confirmed Mary's worst fears. "Do you have someone you can call to be with you?" he'd asked.

Mary's husband had died over twenty years ago, and they'd been too busy traveling and working to have children. Her two siblings, being much older than Mary, had also died earlier, and she'd lost touch with her nieces and nephews over the years. She had no idea where she would spend her final days — maybe weeks if she were lucky — but she dreaded the idea of dying alone in the hospital.

Then the phone call came. It was a voice from Mary's distant past, a voice she hadn't heard in over fifty years. Sharon McGuire had been Mary's best friend from the time they were in first grade. They'd remained in touch for a few years after Mary and Jim had married and moved away, but Mary hadn't seen, or even thought of Sharon, in years.

Somehow Sharon had heard about Mary's illness, and tracked her down at the hospital, and reached out to her. When Mary shared that she had just weeks left, Sharon invited Mary to stay with her in her home, back in Jericho. Sharon had never left, had never married, and was still living in her childhood home.

So here she was, in a room with a view of the mountains of northern Vermont, covered with Mother Nature's glorious and riotous colors of fall. A room in a house filled with childhood memories of birthday parties, sleepovers, stolen kisses, and more.

Sharon had placed a picture of the two of them, arms entwined, laughing at life the way only seventeen-year-old girls could. So many years had passed since that day, and now Mary and Sharon, eighty-two-year-old women, once again shared their lives, in a place where Mary had once lived, a place where she had now come to die.

Gertrude
The Faulty Faucet

Gertrude barely has enough strength to turn off the faucet on the kitchen sink when it works properly. Over the past few weeks, it has become increasingly more difficult to turn it off after washing up her few dishes from her small meals. Yesterday she had thought briefly about calling the plumber, but decided she couldn't afford the cost of his visit. So today she struggles  once again with that darn old faucet. It is after all, as old as this old house – the house she had arrived at after her wedding all those many years ago.

When James had been alive, he took care of things like stubborn faucets, furnaces that wouldn't start, and the like. As so often happened lately, thinking of James, and his death a year ago after a three-year struggle with cancer, brings tears to her eyes, tears that are as difficult to shut off as her cranky old faucet.

Gertrude sighs as she shuffles across the cracked linoleum floor in her pink mules. Like so much else in her life that had once sparkled and seen better days, the linoleum that she and James had so lovingly picked out and installed themselves was now faded and lackluster. As she approaches the sink with her breakfast dishes, having finished her breakfast of cold cereal and orange juice, she again sighs deeply as she turns the water on. After washing up the dishes, and trying unsuccessfully to turn the water off, she exclaims, "Damnation, now I have no choice, I HAVE to call the plumber!"

And tears of frustration begin to flow in concert with the water from the tap as she shuffles to the phone in the hallway.

Maude
The Whistling Tea Kettle

The teakettle had been whistling for over five minutes by the time Maude finally made her way into the kitchen.

"All right, all right, I hear you!" she muttered, as her walker scraped along the old linoleum floor. That floor had been put down more years ago than she could remember, and the once bright pattern had faded to a dull gray.

When, as a new bride, she had moved into her husband's family farmhouse, the kitchen had been the domain of her mother-in-law. After Henrietta died, Maude had in turn ruled the kitchen with a loving hand. Fresh bread every day, pot roast for Sunday dinners after church, milk and chocolate chip cookies for her five children when they came home from school – she had loved every minute of it, and her kitchen had sparkled!

Now, of course, with Harvey gone these past twenty years, and her children, grandchildren and great-grandchildren living far from the farm, Maude relied on Meals-On-Wheels from town for her main meal each day, though she usually found them unsatisfying compared to the meals she used to make.

Three times a week Nancy Walker's daughter Susan would stop by to tidy up the house, although her standards of cleanliness and Maude's were a tad different. She would also sit and have a cup of tea with Maude and tell her about the happenings in town.

In fact, Susan was late today. She was usually very punctual, which is why Maude had put the kettle on and then made her way slowly into the living room to sit in her recliner, out of breath from just that little bit of exertion. So now the kettle continued to whistle its impatience as Maude slowly retraced her steps from the living room, through the dining room, into the kitchen at the back of the house.

As she entered the kitchen, exhausted from her trip in from the front room, she suddenly felt light-headed, and collapsed into the chair at the old wooden table, the table that had been the scene of so many pleasurable meals. She was unable to muster the energy needed to go even the few steps to the stove, but thought to herself, "I'll just sit here for a minute, just until I catch my breath."

And that's where Susan found her – the teakettle still sounding its clarion call.

Thomas
A Trip to The Seashore

Thomas hadn't been to the seashore for many years. As a young man, he had spent all his growing up summers at his grandparent's cottage on the Cape. The summers seemed endless back then. Now they seemed but an eye-blink.

So for his niece Stefanie and her husband Tim to call and let him know they were coming down to Natick from Concord, New Hampshire to take him to the South Shore for the day was a much-appreciated break in the often-dreary days at the Pinecrest Nursing Home.

Connie, the recreation director, tried to get folks interested in things like arts and crafts activities, Bingo, paint-by-numbers, and bowling, but most people seemed to stay in their rooms, coming out only for meals. Thomas would have liked to take advantage of the recreational activities, but with his failing eyesight and wheelchair confinement, it was difficult.

As he sat in the foyer awaiting Stefanie and Tim's arrival, his mind wandered, as it was wont to do, back to those early days at the Cape. He could almost smell the salt sea air of the backshore at Newcomb Hollow and the earthy smell of the wet sand where the waves had danced. The cry of the gulls overhead, wings spread as they soared and floated on the invisible airways, had always seemed to Thomas such a lonely sound.

"Uncle Thomas, we're here," a familiar and much-loved voice brought him back to the present. Thomas had never married, had no children of his own, but Stefanie, his younger sister's daughter, had always been close to her uncle. He smiled up at her, a twinkle in his eye as he asked, "did you remember the chocolate?" It was a favorite ritual they'd started when it was he who would bring her the chocolate when he would visit. "Of course! Now, are you ready for our outing? We've brought a wool blanket in case the sea breeze is too strong, and a picnic lunch. We've discovered a beach that has a boardwalk that will let us push your wheelchair almost to the water's edge." Stefanie kept up a chatter as they got Thomas settled in their van, hoisting the wheelchair into the back.

Thomas rested his head on the headrest, readying himself for what might possibly be his last trip to the ocean he loved so much. If his long life had taught him nothing else – he was a man who knew how to make the most out of every moment.

Shirley
Rules!

Shirley hated the nursing home. Not disliked, really hated. She couldn't understand why her children, the ingrates, had insisted she come here. She'd been perfectly fine in her own home! She'd lived there for more years than she could count and done just fine, thank you very much! So she'd fallen a few times, left the pot on the stove a tad too long and locked herself out getting the paper off the porch when it was below freezing. Those things happen. Didn't mean she was ready for the grave, for pity's sake! Didn't mean she had to be locked up here, away from all that was familiar.

In her own home she had eaten when she was hungry (most of the time), gone to bed when she was tired, sat in her favorite green recliner that fit her body so well after so many years; so what if it didn't work all that well. Here, at Maple Rest, there were too damn many rules. Rules about when you could eat, when you had to go to bed, even rules about when you could pee! Imagine being told when she could or couldn't pee! Outrageous!

Why, just last night when the night nurse came in around midnight, just as Shirley was getting out of bed to use the bathroom, she'd scolded Shirley as if she were a child.

"Now, Miss Shirley, ya'll know that when you lay down at night, you don't raise up, even if you has to pee. Ya'll need to call me to help you."

Fiddle-faddle thought Shirley. No one is going to tell me that I can't get myself up to pee! My children, the ingrates, are going to hear about this, if they ever answer their phone. And she drifted off to sleep.

"Tell them," she will say to her daughter.
"Tell them that I can pee when I want to,
 Tell them that I will be leaving here if they talk to me as if I were a child.
Tell them I am a person, not an object to be moved about at their whim.
Tell them I matter, my feelings matter, my wishes matter.
Tell them you are taking me home. Today. Now. Please."

Sydney
A Calming Presence

Sitting alone in the examining room, Sydney feels his heart begin to race. This is supposed to be a routine check-up, his once-a-year Medicare physical, so why is he suddenly so nervous?

As he sits alone in the cool examining room, bare-assed under the ridiculous "gown", Sydney wishes that Doctor Blair, his doctor for forty years, had not retired as June. He trusted Dr. Blair. How can he trust someone younger than his youngest son to know what to do? How can he divulge his greatest worry that there is something seriously wrong, something that makes his heart race even without exertion?

He has now lived longer than his father did, longer than both his uncles and certainly longer than the grandfather he never knew. All of them were felled by a traitorous heart while still in their fifties and sixties. Why should he be any different? Just because he had passed his seventieth birthday last month, does that make him immune to the family "curse"? That's what his mother had always called it, and that's how Sydney had always thought of it.

As these thoughts tumble around inside his mind, he notices a bird at the window, just sitting there, looking in at him. It is a non-descript, small brown bird, but it seems to be looking intently right at him, it's head cocked to one side as if asking a question. For some reason, this little bird is a calming presence, and Sydney feels his racing heart begin to slow down, and a smile crosses his lips.

"Maybe," he thinks, "Maybe I'm the one to finally break the "curse'" and live into a ripe old age."

The bird is gone now, leaving behind a sense of peace and relief. Sydney adjusts himself on the examining table as the door opens and his new doctor, Dr. Browning, walks in, a ready smile on his face.

"Well, Mr. Eaton, and how are we doing today?"

"Young whippersnapper, I am just fine, but I have no idea how YOU are," is what Sydney thinks, but is too polite to say out loud.

Suddenly, without warning, he breaks out in a cold sweat, his heart racing once again, and as waves of pain radiate out from his chest, he thinks that perhaps he has not outrun the family curse after all.

Mrs. Marshall
DNR

The carpeted corridor in the nursing home was dimly lit, with just enough light for the shift nurses to be able to peer into the rooms to make sure the occupants were settled for the night.

Shadows danced in the slight breeze made by Nurse Janie's passing, the squeak of her rubber-soled shoes a counterpoint to the hissing of oxygen machines and the beeping of the monitors. This was the hospice floor – the floor of no return.

During the shift change earlier, she had asked about Mrs. Marshall in room 212. In the past week she'd become quite fond of her charge and was looking forward to another midnight visit. Mrs. Marshall had no family in the area, and at 92 she was resigned to her fate, telling Janie that "it's in God's hands". A heavy smoker for years, her aging lungs were not able to supply her with the oxygen she needed, so the oxygen machine did it for her.

The doctors had noted "DNR" on her chart at her request, and Janie knew it was only a matter of time before

56

she would perhaps come in some night to find the bed empty. But not tonight. Tonight, as usual, Mrs. Marshall was awake, her head turned towards the door in anticipation.

Pausing a moment at the door, Janie glanced behind her, down the dimly lit corridor, then quietly moved to the bedside and took the old woman's thin, vein-riddled hand in her own, and whispered, "Hello, my dear, I'm here."

Uncle Ted
Leave Taking

Turning his head slightly, Ted sees James standing in the doorway of his bedroom. Ted has not heard him come in, lost in thought as he is, but is happy to see his great-nephew. Sensing some hesitation, he lifts one hand off the bed covers, beckoning James to enter. He knows it is not an easy thing for a young man to come to terms with a loved one dying, and wants to make it as easy as possible.

The hospice volunteer had left the room when James entered, to give them time alone to say their goodbyes. James glances nervously around the room, clears his throat and, as he brushes at the tears leaking out his eyes, whispers "I've come, Uncle Ted – mom called me and said I needed to get here if I wanted to be able to say good-bye."

Ted, or Theodore as he'd been known when he was a professor of English at the local college, is the patriarch of James' family. James, his brothers and sisters and their numerous cousins always loved family gatherings at their great-uncle's home, with its inviting front porch rocker shaded by the old sugar maple tree that Ted's father had planted soon after he'd built the house for his new bride. It is the family center, where each year Thanksgiving, Christmas, and birthdays for young and old had all been celebrated around the oak table in the central dining room. Laughter and the sounds of children had echoed throughout the rooms over the years, sounds that Ted could still hear, although now the house stands quiet – only the sound of his labored breathing and the quiet murmurings of the relatives gathering in the downstairs living room breaking the silence

As Ted looks at the young man seated next to the bed, he  realizes how blessed he is to have this time to say his goodbyes; there is a spaciousness to this time of leave-taking that he is grateful to have. Reaching for James' hand, he gives it a small squeeze, and nods his head, ready to say yet one more good-bye.

Felicia
Afternoon Tea

"Follow the threads. A life well lived has many threads." Her grandmother's words from years ago echo in Felicia's head.

"So, which one should I follow today?" she wonders, sitting in her favorite chair, the sunshine streaming in through the bay window massaging her arthritic knees.

Sipping her Earl Gray tea and munching on her favorite ginger cookies, she follows one thread all the way back to when she was living in Germany after the war.

Before war had ripped away all that was familiar, Felicia had made her living as an actress – not a famous actress certainly, but she was able to make a living and people said she was very talented. But all that changed with the war and her subsequent immigration to America in the early 50's.

She had, as had many others, landed in New York City when she was still young enough to be dazzled by the city and all that it offered. She had found a room in the local YWCA, studied English at night and worked as a cleaning woman during the day. It had taken her a few years, but eventually, she had landed a few parts in off, off Broadway productions.

Still sipping her tea, Felicia follows another thread, this one to the audition where she met her husband, Peter. She can't recall what she was auditioning for, but that day her life changed once again, leading to a happy marriage, with two children and a small but fulfilling career in the theater. Her children, grandchildren, and great-grandchildren were precious blessings, all of whom lived close enough to visit her on a regular basis.

A smile lights up her face as she thinks of her family, followed soon after by a tear trickling down her cheek as she remembered yet another thread, this one not so happy. She and Peter had just celebrated their 44th wedding anniversary. Peter had developed a nasty cough and would not take the time to go to the doctors, eventually succumbing to pneumonia. Once gain her life shifted, this time into quiet widowhood.

"Yes," she thinks to herself, "I can follow the threads of a well-lived, well-loved life, all the way to this sunshine filled brownstone where I still enjoy my afternoon tea and cookies."

And she smiles as the doorbell rings, knowing it is one of her family, come to share her afternoon tea party.

Robert
A Roll of the Dice

A simple roll of the dice, or maybe it wasn't all that simple, but like many memories that surfaced these days, Robert couldn't say with any assurance that his memory of the day that he rolled for high stakes was quite accurate. After all, he was looking back to the early 1940's, when he was just a young 'un. Now here he was, alone with his memories.

He'd been looking at some pictures from his past. These days, he never bothered to get out of his pajamas and bathrobe, always wearing his ever-present scruffy brown slippers. He hadn't even bothered to dress for his company today. Maybe he forgot. Or maybe it was just too much effort.

Robert's great-nephew Steven was visiting him, which was rare. Robert's family had been shrinking the past ten or fifteen years, as his three sisters and two brothers had all died. They'd been scattered across the country, but still, it was hard to know that you were the last of your generation even when you hadn't seen each other much in the past thirty years. Even some of his nieces and nephews had passed on recently. Guess that's what happens when you live so long, Robert mused.

Steven and his brother Paul were the only family living anywhere near the nursing home, and they were both busy with their families and their jobs, so they didn't get to visit Robert often. They always called to make sure it was going to be a good day to visit. Lately, Robert's memory had deteriorated to the point where, at times, he was confused and thought they were his brothers.

During today's visit, Steven noticed a picture next to his uncle's chair, a small black and white photograph that he did not recall seeing before.

"Who's this, Uncle Rob?" he asked, showing it to the old man, who took it in his gnarled hands, chuckling as he did so. The picture was a young man, dressed in slick black pants, a white shirt, studded black vest, a wide Stetson on his head, and a gun holster slung across his hips. A devilish grin completed the picture.

"Why that's me, when I was a professional gamblin' gunslinger on the Mississippi River's premier paddleboat, the Star Queen!" he said, as he continued to hold the picture of the young man he had once been.

"What? Are you serious? You have to tell me the story, please!" Steven could not reconcile the man in the picture with his ancient great uncle, and was eager to hear the story.

With a smile on his face, Robert began, closing his eyes as if he were seeing himself as he once was.

"It was the late 1930's, so it certainly wasn't the Wild West, but the riverboat company did a good job giving the Star Queen tourists a feeling of those days, including gunfights and Indian attacks. My job was to bet those tourists on the roll of the dice that I could roll a seven. Occasionally one of the other crew would act like a gunslinger and we'd have a "shoot out", right there on the deck of the river boat!" Robert was lost for a moment in his memories.

"Hired on when I was only 19, it was one of the best jobs I ever had! I loved the constant flow of people, the excitement, and the chance to get paid for gambling. But one day, several years after I first started, I realized that maybe I couldn't avoid the war that was raging in Europe. I really didn't want to enlist, so I decided to leave it to chance."

"What did you do?" queried Steven, enthralled by the story and the image of his uncle as a gunslinger!

"One night, just before we were due to stop in Natchez, and after everyone else had gone to bed, I decided to roll one more time. If I rolled a seven, I'd stay on the boat. If not, I'd enlist the next day. A simple roll of the dice was going to determine my future."

Robert closed his eyes as if reliving that moment; that roll of those dice. After a few minutes, Steven realized that his uncle had fallen asleep, probably tired out from the telling of such an amazing story. He covered him up and left quietly, shaking his head at what he'd heard. He knew he wanted to find out what had happened with that roll of the dice, so he called his brother when he got home.

"Paul, you are not going to believe what I heard today when I went to see Uncle Rob! You've got to go with me tomorrow. You need to hear it for yourself!"

He proceeded to share with Paul a bit of the story and they agreed to meet at the nursing home the next afternoon so Uncle Rob could reveal the outcome of that fateful dice roll.

But early the next morning, just after breakfast, Steven got a phone call from the nursing home. His uncle had died in his sleep, still clutching the picture of the young gunslinging gambler on the Star Queen.

Jason and Cynthia
The Great Escape!

"Careful! Watch out for those fallen branches! Where are you going? Come back on the path with the rest of us. Oh, good heavens, Jason and Cynthia, you two are going to be the death of me! Be careful!"

Jason glanced over his shoulder but kept going after giving Wendy a puzzled look, as if he had no idea who was yelling at him, or why. Cynthia never even turned around, but kept walking, mumbling to herself, paying no attention to Wendy.

When she first decided to take some of the residents for a walk, Wendy, the new Activities Director at Pine Ridge Assisted Living Village, had thought it a good idea. It was a beautiful Indian Summer day in Northern New England, sunny, not too cool, just right for a walk in the woods. Now, when it was too late, she was having second thoughts.

There was a wide, pine-needle strewn path just across the parking lot, kept neat and tidy by the grounds crew so staff and residents could get out of the somewhat sterile environment and out into nature. The path did not go far, and in fact circled around the back of the Village. What Wendy hadn't counted on was the deadfall that must have come down during the rainstorm on Wednesday and hadn't yet been picked up by the grounds crew. Branches, brown leaves still clinging to them, blocked the path.

Wendy, her attention momentarily distracted as she surveyed the obstacle, looked up in time to see Jason and Cynthia wandering off the path, into the woods! Leaving the other three residents with Lucy, her assistant, she started after the two wanderers, calling out to them.

"Careful! Wait right there, I'm coming!"

It was amazing how quickly two elderly people had managed to get so far into the woods, and Wendy felt some measure of anxiety rise up, as she went after them. She finally managed to catch up with them and with a deep sigh and a shake of her head, led them back to where the rest of the group was waiting, having successfully navigated their way to the other side of the fallen branches.

Jason smiled, as he held out his hand to Cynthia.

"Wasn't that fun?" he whispered. "Shall we run away together again tomorrow?"

Cynthia took his hand, and whispered back, "Why not? What else is there to do?"

Jason chuckled. "They think we are too old and feeble-minded to plan an escape, but we almost made it today, didn't we?"

And hand in hand, they ambled down the path, leaving Wendy to wonder what they had been talking about. With another deep sigh, she led them out of the woods, and back to safety.

Susan
Sunrise Over the Pond

Sunrise was Susan's favorite time of day, always had been ever since she was a little girl growing up in a small town in Rhode Island near Narragansett Bay. She loved waking up about an hour before the sun spread a delicious glow across the pond outside her window. This time of year the Canada geese often rested on the pond on their way north, so Susan always left bread crumbs out along the pond's edge for them.

But this morning the pond was empty. She donned her bathrobe and slippers and made her way down the stairs. After putting the kettle on for tea, she opened the curtains in the living room. When she and Dan had been building their house years ago, she had insisted upon an east facing living room with an extra-large picture window so she could sit and look over the pond in all seasons. Over the years, they had watched the snow fall, the autumn leaves floating down from the maple trees, and see the first buds on the lilac bushes along the stonewall in May. It was her favorite room in the house.

In the winter she and Dan used to curl up together on the couch in front of the fireplace, steaming hot cocoa in their mugs, and share their hopes and dreams for their future retirement. That future together had ended the day Susan answered the phone to hear Sheriff Thompson on the other end. Dan has suffered a heart attack at work and was gone.

Susan managed to get through that first week or two with the help of her extended family, her friends, and neighbors, but after everyone went back to their own lives, she was left to pick up the pieces of her life – alone now.

That had been almost fifteen years ago. Time had dampened the pain, but every now and then she would catch herself wanting to tell Dan something she'd done that day, and it would still take her breath away to realize he was gone.

Today was her birthday, and her one wish had been that the sunrise would be particularly spectacular this morning. She needed the deep reds, the vibrant hues of yellow and orange, under lit with a faint pinkish gold. She needed the colors, the brightness, the hope the sunrise promised. Maybe then the diagnosis she had received yesterday could begin to settle in and be real. Maybe. If she were to be surrounded by one amazing, brilliant sunrise over her pond, the surely everything would be okay, and she would be around for many more sunrises. If not, well, she would just look forward to being with her beloved Dan again.

Sipping her tea, sitting in the comfort of her much-loved living room, she watched as the sun began to peek over the hills, blessing her day. "Another day begins", she thought. "And I'm ready, ready for whatever comes."

Helen
The Phone Call

It was a phone call that precipitated the crisis today. Helen was home alone when the call came, which is unusual. In the seven years since Helen moved in with them, the family always makes sure someone is home with her, just in case she wanders off (she'd done that twice already!), or falls, or any of the other possible scenarios that had arrived along with the heartache of Alzheimer's. When that is not possible, they ask Mrs. Martin, next door, to watch out for her.

On her good days, Helen knows who they all are and can even carry on a simple conversation. But those days have become fewer and fewer, and more often than not, she just sits and rocks the day away, lost in her own wordless world.

Alice, Helen's daughter and major caregiver, remembers the vibrant, strong and loving mother, and is moved to tears when she comes into the living room and sees her mother's vacant eyes pass through her without recognition. Swallowing those tears, she tucks the afghan around her mother's slender body and kisses her on the top of her head. Her mother just rocks. Alice sighs and heads back to the kitchen to wash up the breakfast dishes. Her three teenage children have left for school, and her husband, John, is on his way to the Country Club for a round of golf with his buddies, his major form of escape these days. Alice sits at the kitchen table with a cup of tea, and just for a moment, wonders what her life would be like if her mother were not living with them. She releases another sigh.

"It is what it is, and I love her. I'll make her a chocolate cake for lunch – it's always been her favorite." Alice knows that a chocolate cake won't make it better, but the guilt has crept in again, and it is something she can do.

"Oh dear, I don't have any flour or chocolate! I'll call Mrs. Martin and see if she minds coming over to watch mom while I run to the store."

But Mrs. Martin does not answer her phone. Alice peeks in at her mother, who is now snoring gently. And she makes a decision.

"I'll just be quick – she's fine, she's sleeping and won't even know I've gone." And so saying takes up her keys and purse and heads to the nearby store.

A few minutes after Alice leaves, the insistent ringing of the phone startles Helen awake. She knows she is supposed to do something, so she gets up and reaches for

the phone, but then just stares at it as a disembodied voice comes through the speaker.

"Hello. This is John from the Ford Dealership calling with some exciting news! If you are one of the first ten people to come by our showroom on Washington Avenue within the next hour, you will be eligible for $1000 towards a brand new Ford!

Remember, you need to hurry to claim your chance at $1000!" The robo call ends as suddenly as it had begun.

The phone drops to the floor as Helen excitedly makes her way to the front door. She has no idea where Washington Avenue is, or even what a Ford is, but somehow the idea of getting some money has triggered a memory, and she is going to go find it!

Alice arrives home to find a police car in her driveway with a very bewildered Helen sitting in the back seat. Neighbors have gathered on the front lawn. Alice hears someone say, "I knew she should be in a home, maybe now they'll see reason." Alice ignores them as she moves quickly towards the police car, where Sargent Brown is waiting for her.

"Mrs. Watson, we got a call from one of your neighbors who saw your mother wandering on the sidewalk two blocks from here. Do you know where she was going? She really shouldn't be left alone, you know. This is the third time we've been called about her."

Alice, tears streaming down her face, helps her mother out of the car. Her mother looks so little, she thinks. When did she get so little? She thanks the Sargent with a nod of her head and leads her mother into the house and settles her into the rocking chair.

"Oh mom, what are we going to do, what are we going to do?" But her mother just keeps rocking and says nothing.

When John and the children are all home, Alice sighs and wearily says, "We need to talk".

Dorothy
Arkansas Farm Girl

One whiff, that's all it took and Dorothy's proper matronly self dropped away and she was once again Dottie, that little ten-year-old Arkansas farm girl, frolicking in the hay barn with her four brothers and her cousins on winter mornings before the big yellow school bus arrived at the end of their driveway.

Frankie, Bobby, Jimmy, Tommy, Susan, and Mattie and she would scramble up the ladder and plop down on the bales of hay, pretending they were cowboys and cowgirls back in the old, wild west days. Their adventures were always accompanied by much giggling and full-out laughter.

They took turns being the "lookout", watching for the school bus, and yelling "BUS!" at the top of their lungs once it crested the hill. The bus had been driven by Mr. Carlton, who actually seemed to enjoy his job and the children, and would even invite them all to his house at the end of the school year to decorate the bus.

A mad scramble down the ladder ensued as they raced to beat the bus's arrival. They always ended up with hay in their hair, strands clinging to their coats and pants, reminders later of the joyful beginning to their day.

Miss Dalton, their teacher, always smiled as the "Wilson Gang" trooped in the one-room schoolhouse. "Good morning," she would greet each one, taking a moment to pick hay out of Dottie's hair or off Mattie's coat. Miss Dalto had also grown up on a farm, not too far from where she taught, and had no doubt experienced the same fun they had before coming to school. She had been Dottie's teacher all the way through the eighth grade when she left teaching to get married. Dottie had never understood why the one thing had canceled out the other!

"Grandmother, are you okay?" asked Thomas, Dorothy's nineteen-year-old great-grandson, feeling a bit anxious at the responsibility he'd been given to get his elderly relative to the family picnic. He had picked her up from Shady Acres, the pleasant assisted living facility where Dorothy now lived, and they had stopped at a roadside farm stand to pick up some watermelons for the picnic. In the field beyond the stand lay several acres of hay drying in the sun, and the smell of the fresh cut hay had wafted through the open window and taken Dorothy away, back to when she was a little girl, playing in the barn.

Thomas' voice brought her back. She sighed as she turned to face him. She was grateful for the glimpse she'd had of her younger, playful, joyful self when she'd been with her brothers and her cousins, but felt the old sadness when she thought of them, all long since departed. "Ah well", she sighed, thinking about the newest arrival to the family she would soon meet. "That is life, after all; beginnings and endings."

And she rolled up her window, leaving the hay field and memories of the past behind.

Josephine
Rainy Days

Rainy days had always made Josephine soul weary. Even as a young girl growing up in Portland Maine, a rainy day brought only lethargy and quiet. She often ensconced herself in the bay window at her parent's house, spending endless hours just watching the raindrops race each other down the window, not even able to summon up enough energy to read one of her favorite books or work on an embroidery project.

Her parents had been concerned, of course, but her mother believed in letting her do what she needed to do and convinced her father to leave her be.

As a young wife and mother, her husband and children learned to just leave her alone on rainy days. Back then she had mustered up the where-with-all to get dressed, make breakfast for her family and see them off to school and work. That was all she accomplished before she gave in and just sat by the window, or napped under the afghan her mother had made her for rainy days. In the bosom of her loving family, she had been cocooned and allowed to disengage and retreat. It was a gift she had relished, aware of how precious it was to have rainy days to just BE.

After her husband died, and her children moved away, she had wondered as she watched the falling rain if the raindrops were the tears of everyone who had ever lived, and she the only witness to those tears. She knew it was fanciful, but how else to explain the deep need to stop everything and just watch the rain fall on the bushes outside the house, on the sidewalks, and most of all, on the window panes. Fanciful, yes, but it had made her smile. She had tried to explain this to her children, but they just nodded and she knew they thought her a tad "off". If her mother had still been alive, she knew she would have understood.

Now her children are back, come from the various places their lives had taken them. Josephine's passing three days ago has brought them back to Portland to say goodbye to the mother they love but never understood. As they gather around the gravesite in Evergreen Cemetery, they smile at one another through their tears, as they think how fitting their mother would think it – for now they understand what she had tried to tell them. Of course, it is raining, and as the drops mingle with their tears, for just a brief moment they can see her watching – the way she had always done on rainy days.

John
Violet Syrup

Perfect clumps of violets grew around the edges of the pristine lawn – the gardeners at the Hollybrook Assisted Living facility made sure those "weeds" didn't invade the lawn itself, but stayed where they belonged, in the gardens.

Catching a glimpse of the violets from his bedroom window, John sighed, remembering how he and Elizabeth wouldn't mow their lawn until all the violets had gone by – a sea of deep violet and white and green nestled among the dandelions in the spring.

"What is the matter with leaving things the way Mother Nature intended?" he sighed to his roommate, who was watching TV in the next bed. But as usual, Harold didn't answer.

Then a smile crept over the contours of John's face, lighting it up.

"Wonder if anyone still makes violet syrup – haven't thought of that in years! My Elizabeth knew how to make it, that's for sure!"

Indeed, Elizabeth had spent hours picking the tiny flowers, then separating the small green tip from the flower until she had several cupfuls. Adding an equal amount of boiling water, she left it overnight and then boiled it with an equal amount of white sugar until it formed a creamy syrup. It had to be white sugar; otherwise, the potion turned a sickly shade of brown.

The final result, a lovely deep shade of purple, was poured into mason jars, labeled and refrigerated, to be enjoyed in small amounts over a glass of ice cubes or a dish of ice cream for the rest of the summer.

"What I wouldn't give for a glass of violet water over ice!" he muttered to Harold, who again did not answer, this time because he had fallen asleep. Looking over at him, John sighed again. "Probably just as well, even when he's awake we have nothing to talk about." Harold at ninety-two was just a few years older than John, but slept most of the time, while John still liked to get up and dressed and sit on the patio in the good weather and the atrium when he couldn't get out.

Thinking of Elizabeth and that violet syrup made John tear up.

"I can't believe it's been ten years. I think I miss her most in the spring time, especially around our anniversary in May."

He chuckled, as another memory of violets surfaced. "She insisted we get married in May, because how else could she carry a bouquet of violets and pansies? I can still see those flowers against the white of her silk wedding dress! She was the most beautiful bride, and I was the luckiest man alive!"

John had spoken out loud, not realizing that the new nurse had entered his room.

"Good morning, Mr. Green, I'm Nurse Jordan." she said as she approached his bed. "Is there something I could do or get for you?" She pretended not to see the sheen of unshed tears.

"Well, yes, actually there is. Will you pick lots of violets for me? And then I'll tell you how to make violet syrup. It would be ever so lovely if you could see your way to do that."

"Well, I guess I could do that this afternoon, after my shift is over. How much would you need?"

"Oh, at least a cupful, probably a bit more, that should be enough," he said delightedly.

Just then the head nurse poked her head in the door, calling to Nurse Jordan. "Elizabeth, can you come along to the nurse's station when you are done in here?"

John was startled. "Elizabeth? Really?" And then he smiled. This was going to work out just fine!

Charlene
God's Waiting Room

Lilacs. Lupines. Tulips. Daffodils. Cherry Blossoms. Johnny-Jump-Ups. Their names came easily to her, much easier than so many other things. Spring had always been her favorite season when she was young – so much hope, so many possibilities. The smells, the colors, the freshness of it all! She smiled, but it was a sad smile. Spring in New England had been glorious. Here in South Florida it was – well – boring. Sameness. Nothing much to distinguish one season from another, except maybe the thermometer.

It had not been her decision to spend the remaining years of their lives here. Jack, her late, hardly lamented husband, had never taken her feelings or her wants or needs into consideration, not in all the sixty-eight years they'd been married. As usual, he had simply announced one day that they were moving to Florida, and told her to start packing. He had called it "God's Waiting Room", and indeed, he had lasted only two years before the cancer had taken him.

That was seven months ago, and while she knew she could move back to New England, there was really no point. They had never had children, had both been only children, so there was nobody up there to go back to. Besides, she wasn't sure her old bones could stand the winters as her blood had "thinned out", as the native Floridians always said.

The park model they had bought when they moved to Naples, small as it was, was getting too much for her to

keep up and there was not much room for her to maneuver her walker without bumping into things. Besides, she hadn't much practice making her own decisions, so she just stayed put where she was, at least for now.

But one decision had been easy! The first thing she had done after Jack died was to have someone come and take his old overstuffed recliner to the dump. She had always hated it – hated the color, hated how much room it took up, hated how small it had made her feel as she sat in her tiny rocker. Yes, that decision was easy, but the bigger ones, if and to where she would move, how she would go about selling the park model, as well as all that a move would entail – they were all too much for her.

Even eating was getting to be too much for her. She had never been a good cook. She got by, but somehow she had never gotten the knack of putting a meal together without burning something, or making too much, or not enough. Of course, Jack had always complained; nothing she <u>ever</u> did was good enough for him. So now she existed on cereal, eggs, peanut butter and jelly sandwiches, and cans of Ensure. She was pretty sure she'd lost weight, but she didn't have a scale, and she really didn't care anyway.

Her husband had never let her make friends, not in New England and not down here. He always declared that she needn't bother herself with others; her job was to take care of him. So now, she sat alone, too tired, too old, and too empty to change a lifetime of aloneness. Guess he'd been right – it was God's Waiting Room, and so that's how she'd spend the last days and months of her life. Waiting. Alone and waiting.

Samuel
One Last Adventure

Samuel was ready. Or so he told everyone who would listen.

"We all have to go sometime," he'd started saying each day. "I've lived a long and fruitful life. I'm ready. I'm tired, so very, very tired. This business of living, especially with this pain, is tiresome. I'm ready."

A writer and lover of poetry, especially when he discovered "found poems" in the pages of "Moby Dick", he had begun in recent days to quote one line, out of context, from Dylan Thomas whenever anyone countered his comment with denial, saying, I'm like those "Grave men, near death, who see with blinding light". Of course he left out the part of "do not go gentle into the night".

For that was exactly what he wanted, to go gently into the dark night of death. Indeed, is it not what we all want at the end, to close our eyes and gently drift off? To lay it all down, take a breath, and let go? Why should Samuel have been any different?

When he told his niece several weeks before he died that he was ready to go, she asked him, "Are you dying?" He had responded in typical Samuel fashion - "We are all dying, from the moment we take our first breath we are on a journey to our last breath!"

He died as he had lived his life, on his terms and in his own time, shockingly fast, but surrounded by things he had loved in his nine decades of life: family members, his art, water views from every window, salt sea air, and the love of family and friends.

While we can only wonder what awaited him, avowed atheist that he was, it brings a smile to imagine him sailing free, his boat carrying him on this great adventure, laughing as the wind filled his sails again.

FINAL WORDS

The Back Story

<u>Sunset Voices</u> were written during facilitated groups of the Amherst Writers and Artists method established by <u>Pat Schneider</u>, who says that "a writer is a person who writes". My then fourteen-year-old daughter wanted to join a writing group a friend of ours was facilitating, and since I had to drive her there and back, I decided to also join the group. I had never really written much besides a few poems, and was immediately taken by the ease at which thoughts flowed out when given a simple prompt!

After a lag of about 12 years, I once again found myself in an AWA group at the Keene State College (NH) C.A.L.L program for seniors, and the stories started flowing once again.

My process is interesting in that I ONLY write when in a group – solitary writing just doesn't work for me for whatever reason. And, I need a prompt from outside myself. I've come to accept that and trust the process. The prompt can be a sentence fragment, a song, some interesting objects on the table, a photograph- it doesn't matter. There is only one story that came outside a writing group, but I was with a friend and we gave each other a prompt.

Once I have the prompt, I sit quietly and soon I have a name, a setting and I go from there. I *see* the person, I *see* what he or she is doing, I *hear* them speaking, I *know* their thoughts.

I write in longhand, and do my editing when I type it up on the computer. I often have no idea where the story is going, or how it will end, and am often surprised by the ending. Other times, I know the beginning and just need to "follow the words" to discover the rest. This process never ceases to amaze me! I have had people ask if these are real people. With two exceptions, they are not. At least not anyone I've known.

But perhaps there is a place where the stories are waiting for someone to be open enough, and trusting enough, to let them flow from the end of the pen. That is what this has felt like as I write. I am not the one doing the writing; rather, the stories have come and are writing themselves. It is as Ruth Foreman wrote in the opening poem:

> *be still and let them find you*
> *they will come when they are ready.*

Whether or not the people are real is not what matters. What matters is that the ***stories*** are real. And so I offer these Sunset Voices: Snapshots at the End of Life – because they need to be read and shared and acknowledged. If these stories touch your heart, make you smile, make you cry, even inspire you to become a hospice volunteer, or join or start a hospice singing group, I would love to hear from you!

rev.dvorah@gmail.com
Keene, New Hampshire

Made in the USA
Middletown, DE
27 August 2016